Elvis Presley Biography

The King Who Never Left the Stage!
KIDS Hubbz

Elvis Presley was born on January 8, 1935, in Tupelo, Mississippi, USA.

Copyright© KIDS Hubbz
@2025

All Rights reserved .No part of this publication may be reproduced,redistributed or transmitted in any form or by any means including photocopying ,recording ,or other electronic or mechanical methods without the prior permission of the publisher ,expect in the case of brief quotations embodied in critical reviews and certain other non commercial uses permitted by copyright I

TABLE OF CONTENTS

What is a Biography Book?

Have you ever wondered what it would be like to walk in someone else's shoes? A biography book is a special kind of story that lets you do just that! It's a true story about someone's life, written so we can learn about who they are, what they've done, and how they've made a difference in the world.

The Boy Who Heard Magic in Music

One day, on his eleventh birthday, everything changed.

In a small, quiet town in Mississippi, where the

trees whispered secrets to the wind and the sun painted golden streaks on the dusty roads, there lived a boy named Elvis. He didn't have much—just a pair of worn-out shoes, a head full of dreams, and a heart that beat to the rhythm of music. But Elvis wasn't just any boy. When he listened to the songs on the radio, something magical happened. The music didn't just play—it danced. It swirled around him like a living thing, filling the room with colors and shapes only he could see.

One day, on his eleventh birthday, everything changed. His mom handed him a gift wrapped in brown paper. It wasn't shiny or big, but when he opened it, his eyes sparkled. Inside was a guitar. Not just any guitar—it felt warm in his hands, almost as if it was alive.

Elvis strummed the strings gently, and for the first time, the music didn't just dance around him. It sang back.

What Elvis didn't know was that this guitar held a secret. A magical secret. And with every chord he played, it would take him on an extraordinary journey to become the King of Rock 'n' Roll.

This is the story of how a little boy with a big dream and a magical guitar changed the world forever.
Are you ready to hear the music? Let's begin.

Chapter 1: The Boy with Big Dreams

In the small, sleepy town of Tupelo, Mississippi, there was a little house with peeling paint and a creaky porch. Inside that house lived a boy named Elvis Aaron Presley. Elvis was just like most kids his age. He had a big smile, bright blue eyes, and a lot of questions about the world. But there was one thing about Elvis that made him different—he loved music more than anything else.
Music wasn't just something he listened to. It was something he felt deep inside, like a warm glow that made his heart race and his feet tap. Elvis heard music everywhere: in the birds chirping outside his window, in the sound of the wind rustling through the trees, and even in the steady rhythm of his mom stirring a pot of soup.
"Music is magic," Elvis would say to his mama, Gladys.

"And one day, I'm going to make my own."
Gladys would smile and ruffle his hair. "You've got a big heart, Elvis, and big dreams to match. Who knows? Maybe one day, the whole world will listen to your music."

Elvis's love for music started in church. Every Sunday, he would sit in the wooden pews, his feet barely touching the floor, and listen to the choir sing. Their voices rose like sunlight through the stained glass windows, filling the room with warmth and hope. Elvis loved how the music seemed to lift everyone's spirits, making even the grumpiest faces break into smiles.

One day, Elvis decided he wanted to join the choir. At first, the other kids laughed. Elvis was small and shy, and no one thought his voice would make much of a difference. But when Elvis opened his mouth to sing, the room went quiet. His voice wasn't just good—it was special. It had a sweet, soulful sound that made people feel something deep inside.

"Boy, you've got a gift," the choir director told him.

From that day on, Elvis never stopped singing. He sang while walking to school, while helping his dad with chores, and even while brushing his teeth. His teachers often caught him humming during lessons, but they couldn't stay mad for long. Elvis's music had a way of making people happy.

But Elvis didn't just want to sing—he wanted to play music too. His family didn't have much money, so buying an instrument seemed like an impossible dream. Still, Elvis couldn't stop thinking about guitars. Every time he walked past the music store in town, he'd press his nose against the window and stare at the shiny guitars hanging inside.

One day, Elvis worked up the courage to step inside. The store smelled like wood and polish, and the walls were lined with instruments of every shape and size. Elvis's eyes landed on a small, simple guitar in the corner. It wasn't the fanciest one, but to Elvis, it was perfect.

"Can I try it?" he asked the shopkeeper.

The shopkeeper, a kind old man with a white beard, handed him the guitar. "Go ahead, son," he said.

Elvis held the guitar carefully, as if it were made of gold. He strummed the strings, and though the sound was clumsy at first, Elvis felt a spark of excitement.

"Someday, I'm going to have a guitar of my own," he whispered to himself.

That day came sooner than Elvis expected. On his eleventh birthday, his mom and dad surprised him with a gift wrapped in brown paper. Elvis tore it open and gasped. There, in his hands, was a guitar.

It wasn't shiny or new, but to Elvis, it was the most beautiful thing he had ever seen.

"Happy birthday, my boy," Gladys said, tears in her eyes. "We saved up to get this for you because we believe in your dreams."

Elvis hugged his parents tightly. "Thank you, thank you, thank you!" he cried.

From that moment on, Elvis and his guitar were inseparable. He named it "Blue," after his favorite color and the soulful songs he loved to sing. Elvis spent every spare moment practicing. At first, his fingers stumbled over the strings, and the notes sounded more like a cat yowling than music. But Elvis didn't give up. He kept practicing until his fingers ached, and slowly but surely, the sounds he made started to sound like real music.

Every evening, Elvis would sit on the porch with Blue and play for his family. Neighbors passing by would stop to listen, clapping and cheering when he finished a song.

"Elvis, you've got something special," one neighbor said.

Elvis grinned. "Thanks, but I'm just getting started."

Even as a young boy, Elvis dreamed big. He didn't just want to play music—he wanted to share it with the whole world. He imagined standing on a big stage, playing his guitar while people cheered and danced.

"I'm going to be a singer, Mama," Elvis said one night as he helped her dry the dishes.

Gladys smiled. "I know you will, son. And when you do, don't forget where you came from."

Elvis nodded. "I won't, Mama. I'll always remember."

And so, the boy with big dreams kept practicing, kept singing, and kept believing. Little did he know, the magical journey of Elvis Presley had only just begun.

Chapter 2: A Gift from the Heart

It was a warm January morning in Tupelo, Mississippi, and Elvis Presley was bubbling with excitement. His eleventh birthday was finally here! The small house he shared with his parents wasn't decorated with balloons or streamers, but there was something in the air that felt special. Elvis woke up early, his feet kicking out of the blankets as he scrambled out of bed.

"Mama! Daddy! I'm eleven today!" he called out, his voice ringing through the house.

His mother, Gladys, smiled as she stirred the oatmeal on the stove. "I know, my sweet boy. Eleven years old and already dreaming bigger than anyone in town!"

Elvis grinned and plopped down at the table. He had always been a dreamer. Whether it was singing at church or listening to music on the family's old radio, Elvis believed that music had the power to change lives.

"Do you think I'll get a present this year?" he asked, trying to hide the hope in his voice.

His father, Vernon, glanced at Gladys and gave a small, secretive smile. "You'll just have to wait and see, son."

After breakfast, Elvis went outside to play. As he ran through the dusty streets with his friends, he couldn't stop thinking about what his parents might have planned. Elvis didn't expect anything fancy—his family didn't have much money. Most of the time, birthdays were celebrated with hugs, a warm meal, and a simple prayer of thanks.

But deep down, Elvis wished for something more this year. He had been dreaming about it for months: a guitar. Every time he passed the music store in town, he couldn't help but stare at the guitars in the window. He imagined strumming the strings, making music that would make people smile and dance.

That afternoon, when Elvis came home, his parents were waiting for him in the living room. There was a package on the table, wrapped in plain brown paper. Elvis's eyes widened.

"Is that... for me?" he asked, hardly daring to believe it.

"Of course, it's for you," Gladys said, her eyes twinkling. "Go on, open it!"

Elvis tore into the wrapping like a whirlwind, and when he saw what was inside, his heart skipped a beat. It was a guitar. Not shiny or brand new, but a simple, sturdy acoustic guitar with a smooth wooden finish.

His mouth fell open. "Is this really mine?"

Vernon nodded. "We saved up for it, son. We know how much music means to you."

Elvis ran his fingers over the strings, feeling the vibrations hum through his hands. "Thank you, Mama! Thank you, Daddy! It's the best gift ever!"

Tears welled up in Gladys's eyes as she hugged him. "You're going to do great things with this guitar, Elvis. I just know it."

Elvis couldn't wait to start playing. He rushed to the porch and sat down, cradling the guitar like it was a treasure. But when he strummed the strings, the sound wasn't exactly what he had imagined. It was clunky and out of tune, and his fingers felt clumsy as they tried to press the strings.

He frowned. "It's harder than I thought."
Vernon chuckled and joined him on the porch. "Anything worth doing takes practice, son. Don't give up."

Elvis nodded, determined. Over the next few weeks, he spent every spare moment practicing. At first, it was slow going. His fingers ached from pressing the strings, and more than once, he felt frustrated. But every time he thought about giving up, he remembered his parents' smiles when they gave him the guitar. They believed in him, and he didn't want to let them down.

One evening, as the sun dipped low in the sky, Elvis sat on the porch again, strumming his guitar. This time, something magical happened. The notes started to come together, forming a simple tune. His fingers moved more smoothly, and the music felt alive.

"Mama! Daddy! Listen to this!" he called out.

Gladys and Vernon stepped outside, their faces lighting up as Elvis played his first song. It wasn't perfect, but it was full of heart.

"That's beautiful, Elvis," Gladys said, her voice full of pride. "You've got a gift, my boy."

Elvis beamed. "It's because of you and Daddy. This guitar means everything to me."

From that day on, Elvis and his guitar were inseparable. He named it "Blue," because it reminded him of the soulful music he loved to listen to on the radio. Every evening, he would sit on the porch and play, drawing a small crowd of neighbors who stopped to listen.

"Elvis, you've got something special," one neighbor said, clapping along.

Elvis grinned. "Thanks, but I'm just getting started!"

The gift from his parents wasn't just a guitar—it was a symbol of their love and belief in him. With every note he played, Elvis felt that love, and it gave him the courage to dream even bigger.

Little did he know, this simple guitar would be the start of an incredible journey. A journey that would take him from the porch of his small house in Tupelo to stages all over the world.

And it all began with a gift from the heart.

Chapter 3: Strumming Through Struggles

Elvis Presley sat on the edge of the porch, his guitar resting on his lap. The golden rays of the setting sun stretched across the dusty yard, but Elvis wasn't looking at the sky. His fingers hovered over the guitar strings, and his face was scrunched up in frustration.

"No, that's not right," he muttered as he tried to strum a simple tune.

For weeks now, Elvis had been practicing every day. His parents had given him the guitar for his birthday, and he was determined to make music with it. But learning to play wasn't as easy as he thought it would be. His fingers often stumbled, and the sounds he made didn't match the songs he heard on the radio.

Elvis sighed and leaned back. "Maybe I'm just not good enough," he said to himself.

Just then, his mom, Gladys, stepped out onto the porch with a glass of lemonade. She handed it to him and sat down beside him.

"What's on your mind, honey?" she asked.

Elvis shrugged. "I've been trying so hard, Mama, but I can't get it right. The sounds don't feel like me. I don't think I'll ever be as good as the people on the radio."

Gladys put her arm around his shoulders. "Oh, Elvis. Every great musician starts just like you—trying, learning, and sometimes struggling. But you've got something special, something no one else has."

"What's that?" Elvis asked, looking up at her.

"Your heart," she said, smiling. "When you play, you don't just make noise. You put your feelings into the music. That's what makes it yours."

Elvis thought about that as he sipped his lemonade. Maybe Mama was right. Maybe he didn't need to sound like everyone else. Maybe he just needed to find his own way of playing.

The next day, Elvis decided to try something different. Instead of copying the songs he'd heard, he started making up his own little tunes. They were simple at first—just a few chords and a melody—but they felt more natural. He played with a rhythm that made his feet tap, and sometimes he added words about his life in Tupelo, his family, or his dreams.

One afternoon, while Elvis was strumming away in the backyard, an old neighbor named Mr. Jenkins walked by. Mr. Jenkins was a retired musician who used to play in bands when he was younger. He stopped and listened for a moment before calling out, "You've got some spark in you, boy. Mind if I show you a thing or two?"

Elvis's eyes lit up. "Really? That would be amazing!"

Mr. Jenkins sat down and took the guitar from Elvis. He showed him how to hold it just right and how to strum with more control. Then he taught Elvis a new chord and showed him how to blend it into his songs.

"Music is like telling a story," Mr. Jenkins said. "You've got to feel it, not just play it. Let the guitar speak for you."

Elvis practiced everything Mr. Jenkins taught him. His fingers still stumbled sometimes, and there were days when he got frustrated and wanted to quit. But every time he felt like giving up, he remembered his mom's words and the encouragement from Mr. Jenkins.

As the weeks went by, Elvis started to notice a change. His playing became smoother, and his music started to sound more like him. It wasn't fancy or polished, but it had heart. When he played, his songs felt alive, like they were telling a story that only he could tell.

One evening, while Elvis was playing on the porch, a group of kids from the neighborhood gathered to listen. They clapped along and cheered after each song.

"Wow, Elvis! That was so good!" one of the kids said.

"Yeah," another added. "Your music makes me want to dance!"

Elvis felt a swell of pride. He had worked hard to find his sound, and now people were enjoying it.

"Thanks, y'all," he said with a grin. "I've still got a lot to learn, but I'm not giving up."

As the years went by, Elvis continued to practice and experiment with his music. He listened to everything he could—blues, gospel, country, and even the upbeat rhythms of rock 'n' roll. He took bits and pieces from all these styles and blended them into something unique.

Sometimes, when he hit a tough patch, he'd remember the struggles he faced as a boy learning to play. Those struggles had taught him an important lesson: that it's okay to stumble as long as you keep going.

And so, Elvis kept strumming, kept singing, and kept dreaming. Little by little, he was building something extraordinary—a sound that was truly his own.

What Elvis didn't know yet was that this sound would one day change the world. But for now, he was just a boy with a guitar, strumming through the struggles and finding the music in his heart.

Chapter 4: The Magical Guitar's Secret

Elvis sat cross-legged on the wooden porch, his guitar, Blue, resting in his lap. The sky above Tupelo was painted in streaks of pink and orange as the sun dipped low. It was his favorite time of day—a time when everything felt calm, and the world seemed to listen.

He strummed a soft melody, letting the notes drift into the warm evening air. But tonight, something strange happened. As the sound floated away, it seemed to shimmer, almost as if it were alive. Elvis paused and stared at his guitar.

"That's odd," he murmured. "It never sounded like that before."

He strummed again, a little harder this time. The music sparkled, glowing faintly in the twilight. Elvis leaned closer to Blue, his heart racing.

"Did you... just glow?" he asked the guitar, half-expecting it to answer.

Of course, the guitar stayed silent, but Elvis couldn't shake the feeling that something special was happening. He ran inside, clutching Blue.

"Mama! Mama!" he called out, breathless.

Gladys looked up from the sewing she was working on. "What is it, Elvis? You look like you've seen a ghost!"

"It's not a ghost, Mama," he said, holding up the guitar. "I think Blue has magic in it!"

Gladys smiled and shook her head. "Magic? Oh, Elvis, you've always had an imagination. Maybe it's just your music getting better."

But Elvis wasn't convinced. He knew what he had seen. Determined to find out more, he decided to keep playing and see if the magic would happen again.

The Whispering Strings

The next day, Elvis took Blue out to the backyard. He sat under the shade of a big oak tree and began to play. He started with a simple tune, his fingers moving over the strings. At first, everything seemed normal. But then, as he hit a high note, the strings gave off a soft hum, almost like they were whispering.

Elvis froze. He leaned in, his ear close to the guitar. The hum wasn't just a sound—it was a melody, faint but clear. It wasn't coming from the strings; it was coming from somewhere deep inside the guitar.

"What are you trying to tell me, Blue?" Elvis whispered.

The hum grew louder, and suddenly, Elvis felt a strange warmth spread through his hands. It wasn't uncomfortable—it felt... good. Like the music was wrapping around him, filling him with energy and joy.

He started to play again, and this time, something incredible happened. The notes seemed to leap out of the guitar, swirling through the air like tiny sparks of light. The music wasn't just something to hear—it was something to see and feel.

Elvis laughed in amazement. "You *are* magic!"

A Visit from Mr. Jenkins

Later that afternoon, Elvis ran to find Mr. Jenkins, the retired musician who had been teaching him chords.

"Mr. Jenkins, you won't believe this!" Elvis said, bursting into the old man's yard.

"What's got you all fired up, boy?" Mr. Jenkins asked, setting down the harmonica he had been playing.

"It's my guitar! It's got magic in it!"

Mr. Jenkins raised an eyebrow. "Magic, you say? Well, let me see."

Elvis handed him Blue and watched as Mr. Jenkins strummed a few chords. The notes were smooth, but nothing unusual happened.

"Hmm," Mr. Jenkins said, handing the guitar back. "Sounds like a good guitar to me, but I don't see any magic."

Elvis frowned. "But I saw it! The music sparkled, and the strings whispered a melody I didn't play!"

Mr. Jenkins leaned back in his chair, his eyes twinkling. "Maybe the magic only shows itself to you, Elvis. Ever think of that? Maybe this guitar knows you've got something special in your heart, and it's helping you bring it out."

Elvis thought about that all the way home. Could Mr. Jenkins be right?

The Secret Comes Alive

That evening, Elvis sat on his porch again, cradling Blue. He closed his eyes and strummed softly. This time, he didn't try to force anything. He just let the music flow, playing what felt right.

As he played, the magic returned. The notes shimmered, and the air around him seemed to hum with life. Suddenly, he felt a strange pull, like the guitar was guiding him.

Images began to form in his mind—bright stages, cheering crowds, people smiling and dancing to his music. It was as if the guitar was showing him glimpses of the future.

Elvis stopped playing, his hands trembling. "You're trying to tell me something, aren't you, Blue?" he whispered.

The guitar hummed softly in response.

That night, Elvis couldn't sleep. He kept thinking about the magic in his guitar and the images it had shown him. He didn't know exactly what it all meant, but he felt a spark of determination light up inside him.

"I'm going to keep playing, Blue," he said. "I'm going to follow the music wherever it takes me."

A Magical Journey Begins

From that day on, Elvis practiced harder than ever. He experimented with different chords and rhythms, letting the magic guide him. The guitar didn't always glow or hum, but every now and then, it would remind him of its secret—a flicker of light, a soft whisper, a warm feeling in his hands. Elvis began to believe that the magic wasn't just in the guitar—it was in him too. Blue had simply helped him find it.

And so, with his magical guitar by his side, Elvis set out on a journey that would one day make him the King of Rock 'n' Roll. But for now, he was just a boy with big dreams, a little magic, and a heart full of music.

Chapter 5: Singing at Sun Studio

Elvis Presley couldn't believe his eyes as he stood outside Sun Studio in Memphis, Tennessee. The modest brick building didn't look like much from the outside, but inside, magic happened. This was where some of his favorite musicians had recorded their songs, and now it was his turn. He clutched his guitar, Blue, tightly and took a deep breath. His palms were sweaty, and his heart was pounding. What if they didn't like his singing? What if he wasn't good enough?

"Don't worry, Elvis," his mom, Gladys, had said before he left home that morning. "You've got something special in you. Just be yourself, and they'll see it too."

Her words echoed in his mind as he pushed open the door and stepped inside.

A Nervous Beginning

Inside the studio, Elvis was greeted by a man named Marion Keisker, the assistant to Sam Phillips, the owner of Sun Studio. She had a kind smile and seemed genuinely interested in what Elvis had to say.

"Hi there," she said. "What can I do for you?"

Elvis cleared his throat. "I'd like to record a song. It's... um... for my mama."

Marion smiled wider. "Well, aren't you sweet? Come on in. Let's get you set up."

Elvis followed her into the recording room. It was small but filled with all kinds of equipment—microphones, cables, and a big console with blinking lights. Elvis had never seen anything like it before.

"Go ahead and get ready," Marion said, motioning to a microphone. "Sam's out right now, but I'll help you get started."

Elvis nodded and unpacked his guitar. His hands shook as he tuned the strings. He glanced at Marion, who was watching him with encouraging eyes.

"You can do this," he whispered to himself.

The First Notes

Elvis stepped up to the microphone, closed his eyes, and began to sing. He chose a simple song—a ballad his mom loved to hear him play at home. His voice was soft at first, but as he got into the music, it grew stronger.

The sound filled the room, rich and full of emotion. Marion stopped what she was doing and stared at Elvis. She hadn't expected this shy young man to have such an incredible voice.

When he finished the song, there was a moment of silence. Elvis opened his eyes, his face red with embarrassment. "Was that okay?" he asked.

Marion broke into a grin. "Okay? That was amazing, Elvis! You've got something really special."

Elvis felt a wave of relief and pride. Maybe his mom was right—maybe he did have something worth sharing.

Sam Phillips Hears the Magic

Later that day, Sam Phillips returned to the studio. Marion couldn't wait to tell him about Elvis. "You have to hear this boy," she said, practically dragging Sam into the recording room.

Elvis was still there, sitting on a stool and strumming his guitar. He looked up nervously as Sam walked in.

"So, you're the one Marion's been raving about," Sam said, raising an eyebrow.

"Yes, sir," Elvis said, his voice barely above a whisper.

"Well, let's hear what you've got," Sam said, crossing his arms.

Elvis stood up, adjusted the microphone, and began to sing again. This time, he chose a more upbeat song, tapping his foot as he played. His voice was smooth yet powerful, and there was something in the way he sang that made the music come alive.

Sam's eyes widened as he listened. He leaned closer, studying Elvis as if trying to figure out what made him so special. When the song ended, Sam let out a low whistle.

"Kid, you've got a voice like no one else," he said. "It's raw, it's different, and it's exactly what I've been looking for."

Elvis blinked. "Really? You mean that?"

"I do," Sam said. "You've got something unique, Elvis. With the right song, you could really make people sit up and listen."

A Surprise Recording

Sam decided to record Elvis singing a few songs to see what he could do. They tried some ballads and country tunes, but something was missing. Elvis sang beautifully, but the spark Sam was looking for wasn't quite there.

Then, as they were about to call it a day, Elvis started messing around with his guitar. He strummed a fast, playful rhythm and began singing a fun song called "That's All Right."

Sam's head shot up. "What's that?" he asked.

"Oh, it's just something I like to play for fun," Elvis said, stopping mid-song.

"Don't stop!" Sam said, his eyes lighting up. "Keep going!"

Elvis grinned and launched back into the song. This time, he let loose, moving with the music and pouring all his energy into the performance. Marion clapped along, and even Sam tapped his foot.

When Elvis finished, Sam jumped up. "That's it!" he said. "That's the sound I've been looking for!"

A Star in the Making

The recording of "That's All Right" became Elvis's first official song. When it was played on the radio a few days later, people couldn't get enough of it. Calls flooded in from listeners asking, "Who is that singer?"

Elvis couldn't believe it when he heard his own voice on the radio. "Mama, they're playing my song!" he shouted, running through the house. Gladys hugged him tightly. "I knew you could do it, Elvis. I knew you had something special."

From that moment on, Elvis's life began to change. He wasn't just a boy with a dream anymore—he was on his way to becoming a star. And it all started with one magical day at Sun Studio, where he found his voice and surprised everyone, including himself.

Chapter 6: Becoming the King

The little boy from Tupelo, Mississippi, had come a long way. Elvis Presley, with his guitar, Blue, and his unmistakable voice, was no longer just a local talent. His music was spreading across the country like wildfire, and people everywhere were starting to recognize his name. But how did this shy young man become "The King of Rock 'n' Roll"?

The Radio Revolution

After recording "That's All Right" at Sun Studio, Elvis's song was played on the local Memphis radio station. As soon as it hit the airwaves, phones began ringing nonstop. People couldn't get enough of the new sound.

"Who is that singing?" callers asked. "Play it again!"

The DJs were amazed. They played the song three times in a row, something they'd never done before. Each time, more people called in, wanting to know more about this young man with the soulful voice and catchy rhythm.

For Elvis, hearing his song on the radio for the first time felt like a dream. He had worked so hard, and now people were finally hearing what he had to offer.

"It's only the beginning," Sam Phillips told him. "You're going places, Elvis."

The First Big Shows

Soon, Elvis started performing in front of bigger crowds. At first, he was nervous. Standing on stage with all those eyes on him made his knees shake. But when he began to sing, something incredible happened. The music took over, and the nerves disappeared.

Elvis didn't just stand still and sing like most performers. He moved with the music, swaying and tapping his feet. His energy was contagious, and the audience couldn't help but cheer.

At one show, something unexpected happened. As Elvis danced on stage, the girls in the audience started screaming. They clapped, cheered, and even cried as he performed. Elvis was startled at first, but he quickly realized that his unique style and charm had struck a chord with the crowd.

"Looks like you've got yourself some fans," Sam said with a chuckle after the show.

Elvis blushed. "I was just having fun."

"Well, keep having fun," Sam said. "The people love it!"

The Big Break

In 1956, Elvis got his big break. He signed with RCA Records, a major music label that helped his music reach even more people. His first song with RCA, "Heartbreak Hotel," became a huge hit. It topped the charts and introduced Elvis to the rest of the country.

Television soon came calling, and Elvis made his first appearance on *The Ed Sullivan Show*, one of the most popular shows in America. That night, millions of people tuned in to watch the young singer perform.

Elvis sang his heart out, his voice powerful and full of emotion. But it wasn't just his singing that grabbed everyone's attention—it was the way he moved. His dancing was unlike anything people had seen before. Some called it daring, while others thought it was just plain fun.

No matter what people thought, one thing was clear: Elvis had become a sensation.

A New Sound

What made Elvis stand out wasn't just his voice or his dancing—it was the music itself. He blended different styles, from blues and gospel to country and rock 'n' roll, creating something entirely new. "Your music doesn't fit into just one box," Marion Keisker told him. "That's why people love it. It's something they've never heard before."

Elvis knew that his sound was special, but he also knew it came from the heart. Every song he sang was a piece of his story, a reflection of his journey from a small-town boy to a rising star.

Fame and Challenges

As Elvis's popularity grew, so did the challenges. He was traveling constantly, performing in different cities almost every night. The long hours were exhausting, and he often missed being home with his family.

There were also critics who didn't like his music or his dancing. Some thought he was too different, too bold. But Elvis didn't let the negativity stop him.

"I'm just being myself," he told his mom one evening. "I'm singing the way I feel and moving the way the music moves me. That's all I can do." Gladys smiled and hugged him. "That's why people love you, Elvis. You're not pretending to be anyone else."

Crowning the King

By the late 1950s, Elvis was no longer just a popular singer—he was a phenomenon. His records sold millions of copies, his movies drew huge crowds, and his concerts were packed with fans who couldn't get enough of him.
The newspapers began calling him "The King of Rock 'n' Roll," a title that made Elvis laugh.
"I don't feel like a king," he said. "I'm just Elvis."
But to his fans, he was more than just Elvis. He was someone who brought joy, energy, and excitement into their lives. His music made them feel alive, and his story inspired them to dream big.

A Legacy of Music

As the years went by, Elvis continued to make music, each song filled with the same passion and heart that had made him famous. He never forgot where he came from or the people who had supported him along the way.

"Every note I play, every song I sing, it's for the people," Elvis said. "They're the ones who made this possible."

And so, Elvis Presley, the boy from Tupelo who once doubted himself, became a legend. His journey wasn't always easy, but he faced every challenge with courage and determination. Through his music, he changed the world—and that's why, even today, he's remembered as *The King*.

Chapter 7: Blue Suede Shoes and Bold Moves

Elvis Presley loved music, but he also loved style. From the way he dressed to the way he moved on stage, Elvis always found a way to stand out. One

of his most iconic moments came with the song "Blue Suede Shoes," a song that became a hit not just for its catchy tune but for the bold moves Elvis created to go along with it.
But how did Elvis come up with his famous style and dance moves? Let's find out.

A Song with a Message

"Blue Suede Shoes" wasn't originally written by Elvis. It was written by a musician named Carl Perkins, who was a friend of Elvis's. The song had a fun, upbeat rhythm and a unique message: no one should ever step on a man's blue suede shoes!
Elvis loved the song the first time he heard it. He thought it was playful, full of energy, and just the kind of tune that made people want to dance. When he recorded his own version, Elvis added his special touch, giving the song a fresh and exciting vibe.
But Elvis didn't just sing the song—he brought it to life.

Discovering His Moves

Elvis had always been full of energy, even as a kid. When he listened to music, he couldn't help but tap his feet, sway his hips, and clap along to the beat. It was as if the music took control of his body, and he loved every second of it.

When Elvis began performing on stage, he didn't think about what he looked like. He just moved the way he felt. But his natural rhythm and unique movements quickly caught people's attention.

One night, during a small concert, Elvis was performing "Blue Suede Shoes." As he sang the lyrics, he tapped his feet and slid across the stage, mimicking someone trying to keep their shoes clean. The crowd erupted in laughter and cheers.

Encouraged by their reaction, Elvis added more playful moves. He swayed his hips, twisted his legs, and even bent his knees to the beat. The audience couldn't get enough of it.

"Do that move again!" someone shouted from the crowd.

Elvis grinned and repeated the motion, spinning on his heels and pointing to his imaginary blue suede shoes. The crowd went wild.

The Bold Moves Get Bolder

As Elvis performed more shows, his moves became bolder and more creative. He realized that dancing wasn't just about entertaining the audience—it was about expressing the music in a whole new way.

One of his most famous moves involved shaking his legs while keeping his upper body steady. It was a simple yet eye-catching motion that fans began calling the "Elvis leg shake." Whenever he did it, the crowd would scream with excitement.

Elvis didn't stop there. He experimented with spins, knee slides, and even a signature "hip swivel" that became one of his trademarks. Some people thought his dancing was too wild, but Elvis didn't let that bother him.

"I'm just moving the way the music makes me feel," he said. "It's all part of the show."

The Look of a Star

Elvis's bold style wasn't just about his moves—it was also about his clothes. He knew that being a performer meant standing out, and he worked with designers to create outfits that no one would forget.

For his performances, Elvis wore flashy suits with bright colors, rhinestones, and wide collars. He even had special blue suede shoes made just for him! His outfits became just as famous as his music, inspiring fans to copy his style.

But Elvis didn't stop there. He also popularized hairstyles that were sleek and bold, like his famous pompadour—a hairstyle with a big wave in the front. It became a trend, and soon, boys across the country were trying to style their hair just like Elvis.

Not Everyone Approved

While many people loved Elvis's moves and style, not everyone was a fan. Some adults thought his dancing was too wild and that his flashy outfits were too much.

"Why does he have to wiggle so much?" one reporter asked during an interview.

Elvis just smiled and shrugged. "I'm not trying to cause trouble," he said. "I'm just being myself." His fans, especially the younger ones, didn't care what the critics said. To them, Elvis was exciting, fun, and different. He represented a new kind of energy and freedom, and they loved every bit of it.

The Legacy of Blue Suede Shoes

"Blue Suede Shoes" became one of Elvis's most popular songs, but it was more than just a hit—it was a symbol of his boldness and creativity. The song showcased his ability to take something simple and turn it into something unforgettable. Through his dance moves and style, Elvis showed the world that it was okay to be different and to express yourself in your own way. His performances were more than concerts—they were experiences, full of life and energy.

A King in the Making

Elvis's bold moves and unique style helped him stand out from other performers of his time. He wasn't just singing songs—he was creating moments that people would remember forever. As he continued to perform and create music, Elvis's fame grew. But no matter how big he became, he never forgot the joy of just being himself. His dancing, his style, and his music all came from the heart, and that's what made him special.

And so, with a pair of blue suede shoes and a lot of bold moves, Elvis Presley danced his way into history, leaving a legacy that still inspires people today.

Chapter 8: Adventures on Stage

Every time Elvis Presley stepped onto a stage, something exciting was bound to happen. From the moment the spotlight hit him, he wasn't just a singer—he was a performer, ready to entertain his audience with music, dance, and his signature charm. But being on stage wasn't always predictable. In fact, some of Elvis's most unforgettable moments happened when things didn't go as planned!

Let's take a look at some of Elvis's fun and adventurous stories from his time on stage.

The Dancing Guitar

Elvis loved his guitar, Blue, and brought it with him to almost every performance. It was like his partner in music. But one night, during a lively concert, Blue decided to steal the show!

Elvis was in the middle of performing a fast-paced rock 'n' roll song. As he danced across the stage, he swung Blue around his neck, holding it by the strap. The crowd cheered, loving the energy of the performance.

But then, the guitar strap slipped! Blue spun around and landed on the floor with a loud thunk. The audience gasped, thinking the guitar might be broken.

Elvis didn't miss a beat. He bent down, picked up Blue, and held it high in the air like a trophy. "She's still alive!" he shouted with a grin. The crowd erupted in laughter and applause.
From that night on, Elvis made sure to double-check his guitar strap before every show.

The Screaming Fans

Elvis was no stranger to screaming fans. In fact, they were a big part of his concerts. But during one particular performance, the crowd's excitement took on a life of its own.
As Elvis sang one of his biggest hits, a group of fans rushed the stage, desperate to get closer to him. Security tried to hold them back, but one fan managed to grab Elvis's scarf right off his neck! Elvis laughed and handed the fan another scarf he had tucked in his pocket. "Here you go," he said with a wink. "I've got plenty!"
The gesture made the crowd go even wilder, and from that night on, Elvis started bringing extra scarves to his shows. He'd toss them into the

audience as souvenirs, creating a fun tradition that fans loved.

The Wardrobe Malfunction

Elvis was known for his flashy outfits, from rhinestone-studded suits to brightly colored capes. But sometimes, those fancy clothes had a mind of their own.

During one performance, Elvis wore a white jumpsuit with a wide belt. As he danced and moved across the stage, the belt came loose and fell to the floor.

The audience laughed, and so did Elvis. "Well, I guess this outfit wasn't made for dancing!" he joked as he picked up the belt and draped it over his shoulder.

From that point on, Elvis made sure his outfits were as sturdy as they were stylish. Still, he always laughed off any unexpected wardrobe malfunctions, turning them into part of the show.

The Singing Puppy

One of the funniest moments in Elvis's stage career involved an unexpected guest—a tiny puppy! Elvis was performing at an outdoor concert when a little dog wandered onto the stage. The puppy looked up at Elvis and barked, as if trying to join in the music.

The audience roared with laughter, and Elvis couldn't help but smile. He knelt down, petted the puppy, and said, "Looks like we've got ourselves a backup singer!"

The puppy stayed on stage for the rest of the song, wagging its tail and barking along to the beat. After the concert, Elvis made sure the puppy was safely returned to its owner.

The Broken Microphone

One night, during a particularly energetic performance, Elvis's microphone suddenly stopped working. The crowd could see his lips moving, but no sound came out.

Instead of panicking, Elvis turned the situation into a game. He mimed singing, pretending to be an opera singer one moment and a cowboy the next. The audience laughed and cheered, enjoying the playful performance.

Eventually, the microphone was fixed, and Elvis picked up right where he left off. But for many fans, the silent "singing" was the highlight of the show.

The Fan on Stage

Elvis always had a special connection with his fans, and one night, he decided to bring that connection to the next level.

During a concert, he spotted a young boy in the front row who was singing along to every word. Elvis leaned down and said, "Come on up here, kid!" The boy climbed onto the stage, his eyes wide with excitement. Together, they sang a verse of the song, and the audience cheered louder than ever. When the song ended, Elvis gave the boy a high five and said, "You've got the makings of a star!"

It was a moment the young fan—and the audience—would never forget.

The Flying Cape

Elvis loved wearing capes during his performances. They added a touch of drama and made him feel like a superhero. But one night, the cape decided to take on a life of its own.

As Elvis twirled around on stage, the cape flew off his shoulders and landed in the middle of the audience. A lucky fan caught it and held it up like a trophy.

Elvis laughed and said, "Looks like my cape has found a new home!"

The moment became legendary, and fans began hoping they'd be the next to catch a piece of Elvis's costume.

A Performer Who Loved to Laugh

Elvis's adventures on stage showed that he wasn't just a great singer—he was a great entertainer. No matter what happened, he found a way to keep the show fun and exciting.

For Elvis, every performance was a chance to connect with his audience and share his love of music. Whether he was dealing with a broken microphone, a wandering puppy, or a wardrobe mishap, Elvis always made sure his fans left with a smile.

And that's what made him not just a performer, but a legend—someone who could turn even the smallest moments into unforgettable adventures.

Chapter 9: The Mystery of Graceland

When Elvis Presley bought a big, beautiful house in Memphis, Tennessee, he had no idea it would become one of the most famous homes in the world. Named Graceland, it wasn't just a house—it was a magical place full of fun, laughter, and even a few secrets!

Elvis loved his new home and wanted it to be a place where his family and friends could gather, where music filled every corner, and where he could create memories that would last a lifetime. But what made Graceland so special? Let's take a journey through the mysterious and magical world of Elvis's beloved home.

A Dream Come True

When Elvis first saw Graceland, he was just a young man who had recently become famous. He had always dreamed of buying a big house for his family, and Graceland was perfect. It sat on a hill with sprawling green lawns, tall trees, and plenty of space to relax and have fun.
"This is it," Elvis said with a smile. "This is home." He moved in with his parents, Gladys and Vernon, and his beloved grandmother, Minnie Mae. Elvis wanted his family to feel comfortable and happy, and Graceland became a symbol of everything he had worked so hard for.

The Jungle Room

One of the most mysterious and magical parts of Graceland was the Jungle Room. Decorated with green carpets, wooden furniture, and a waterfall, it looked like something straight out of an adventure movie.

Elvis loved spending time in the Jungle Room. It was a place where he could relax, play music, and dream up new ideas. He even recorded some of his songs there, turning the room into a mini recording studio.

Visitors often wondered if there was more to the Jungle Room than met the eye. "Does this waterfall lead to a secret passage?" one of Elvis's friends jokes.

Elvis just laughed. "Maybe it does," he said with a wink.

The Music Room

Graceland wouldn't have been complete without a music room. Elvis filled it with instruments, records, and a shiny grand piano. Whenever guests came over, they were treated to impromptu concerts as Elvis played and sang some of his favorite tunes.

The music room had a special kind of magic. People said that no matter how they were feeling, stepping into the room made them smile.

"Elvis's music isn't just something you hear," one friend said. "It's something you feel."

The Horses of Graceland

Outside, Graceland was just as magical as it was inside. Elvis loved animals, and one of his favorite things to do was ride horses on the property. He even built a stable and filled it with beautiful horses for his friends and family to enjoy. His favorite horse was a golden palomino named Rising Sun, and the two of them spent countless hours exploring the grounds together.
Sometimes, Elvis would ride his horse to the front gate to greet fans who had gathered outside. He'd wave and say, "How y'all doing?" making everyone feel special.

A Place for Fun

Graceland wasn't just a house—it was a playground! Elvis added all kinds of fun features to make it a place where everyone could have a great time.

He built a swimming pool where he and his friends could splash around on hot summer days. He added a racquetball court, where he played games late into the night. And in true Elvis fashion, he even bought a golf cart to zoom around the property. "Elvis was like a big kid," one of his friends said. "He just wanted everyone to have fun."

The Secret Room

Every famous house needs a good mystery, and Graceland was no exception. Rumors swirled about a secret room hidden somewhere in the house. "Does it have treasure in it?" one of Elvis's cousins asked.

Elvis just smiled. "That's for me to know and you to find out."

No one ever found the secret room—if it even existed. But the idea added to the magic of Graceland, making it a place where anything seemed possible.

The Gates of Graceland

The gates of Graceland were unlike any other. Designed with musical notes and silhouettes of Elvis playing the guitar, they welcomed visitors into a world of music and magic.

Fans from all over the world came to see the gates, leaving messages, flowers, and gifts for Elvis. Even after his concerts, Elvis would sometimes stop by the gates to chat with fans and sign autographs.

"It's amazing how much love this place holds," he once said.

A Magical Legacy

Graceland wasn't just a home for Elvis—it was a symbol of his journey, his dreams, and his love for music. It was a place where he could be himself, surrounded by the people and things he cared about most.

Today, Graceland is open to visitors who want to see the magic for themselves. Walking through the halls, standing in the Jungle Room, and looking at Elvis's gold records on the walls, people can feel the spirit of the man who turned a house into a legend.

"Elvis may be gone," one visitor said, "but his magic lives on here at Graceland."

And that's the true mystery of Graceland—not just the secrets it holds, but the way it continues to inspire everyone who visits. Elvis's home is more than a building; it's a reminder that dreams can come true and that music has the power to make the world a little more magical.

Chapter 10: Songs from the Heart

Elvis Presley wasn't just a singer—he was a storyteller. Through his songs, he shared emotions, told stories, and brought people together. Each note he sang came straight from his heart, and that's why his music touched so many people around the world. Whether it was a fun, toe-tapping rock 'n' roll tune or a soulful ballad, Elvis's songs were always full of love and joy.

But how did Elvis use music to spread such happiness? Let's explore how he turned his passion for music into a gift for everyone to enjoy.

A Voice That Stood Out

From the very beginning, Elvis's voice was something special. It had a rich, warm quality that could make people smile, cry, or feel like they were dancing on air. But more than that, Elvis sang with feeling.

When Elvis performed a love song, you could hear the tenderness in his voice. When he sang about heartbreak, it was as if he was sharing his own sadness. And when he belted out a rock 'n' roll hit, his energy was so contagious that listeners couldn't help but dance along.

"Music is about feelings," Elvis once said. "If you can make people feel something, you've done your job."

The Power of Love

One of Elvis's most famous songs was "Can't Help Falling in Love." It was a simple, beautiful melody about falling head over heels for someone special.
When Elvis sang it, his voice carried so much emotion that listeners felt like he was singing just for them.
The song became a favorite at weddings, anniversaries, and special moments between loved ones. It showed that music didn't need to be complicated to be meaningful—it just needed to come from the heart.
Elvis often said that love was one of the most important things in life, and he used his music to remind people of that.

Songs That Made You Dance

Elvis also had a gift for creating songs that made people want to get up and move. Hits like "Hound Dog," "Jailhouse Rock," and "All Shook Up" were full of energy and fun.
When people listened to Elvis's rock 'n' roll songs, they couldn't help but tap their feet, clap their

hands, or twirl around the room. These songs were about joy—pure, simple joy that everyone could share.

"Elvis's music makes you forget your worries," one fan said. "When his songs come on, all you can think about is how good it feels to dance."

Singing for Hope

While many of Elvis's songs were upbeat and fun, he also used his music to bring hope to people who were feeling down. Songs like "If I Can Dream" and "Peace in the Valley" carried messages of hope, faith, and unity.

"If I Can Dream" was especially powerful. Elvis sang it during a time when the world was going through big changes, and people were looking for hope. The song talked about dreaming of a better, brighter future, and Elvis's heartfelt performance moved everyone who heard it.

"Elvis wasn't just singing for himself," a fan said. "He was singing for all of us."

Sharing Joy with Fans

Elvis loved performing for his fans, and he made sure that every concert was a special experience. He would smile, wink, and even joke with the audience, making them feel like they were part of the show.

One of Elvis's favorite things to do was throw scarves into the crowd during his performances. Fans would scream with excitement as they caught these small gifts, feeling like they had received a piece of Elvis's love.

"Elvis had a way of making everyone feel included," a friend said. "It didn't matter who you were or where you came from—when he sang, you felt like you belonged."

A Gift for Everyone

Elvis didn't just perform for big audiences. He also used his music to bring joy to people who needed it most. He often visited hospitals and played for children who were sick, or performed at charity events to help those in need.

One Christmas, Elvis recorded an album full of holiday songs, including the beautiful "Blue Christmas." The album became a favorite for families around the world, spreading the warmth and magic of the season.

"Elvis's music was a gift," one fan said. "He gave it to everyone, no matter where they were or what they were going through."

A Timeless Message

Even though Elvis is no longer here, his music continues to inspire people of all ages. His songs remind us to love one another, to find joy in the little things, and to never stop dreaming.

"Music is something that lives forever," Elvis once said. "As long as it makes people happy, it's doing its job."

And that's exactly what Elvis's music does. Whether you're listening to a heartfelt ballad or a lively rock 'n' roll tune, you can feel the love and joy he poured into every note.

A Heart Full of Music

Elvis's songs weren't just about words and melodies—they were about sharing a piece of himself with the world. Through his music, he showed that love, hope, and happiness are the most powerful things we can share with one another.

And so, every time someone listens to an Elvis song, they're not just hearing music—they're feeling the heart of a man who wanted to make the world a little brighter, one song at a time. And that's a legacy that will never fade away.

CONCLUSION

A long time ago, in a small town called Tupelo, Mississippi, a shy boy named Elvis loved music more than anything. He wasn't rich, he wasn't famous, but he had something special—his voice! As a kid, Elvis listened to gospel songs at church, country tunes on the radio, and blues music in his neighborhood. He saved up money to buy his first guitar and played whenever he could. But at school, he was so quiet that many kids didn't even notice him!

One day, Elvis recorded a song as a gift for his mother. Little did he know that this small moment would change his life forever! A music producer heard his unique voice and invited him to sing more songs. Soon, Elvis was shaking his hips, strumming his guitar, and making crowds go wild!

With his slick hair, dazzling smile, and electrifying dance moves, Elvis became a sensation. People had never seen anything like him before! His rock 'n' roll music made kids jump, dance, and sing along. But not everyone liked his bold moves—some adults thought he was too wild!

Still, nothing could stop Elvis. He starred in movies, performed on the biggest stages, and became known as "The King of Rock 'n' Roll." Even after he left the stage, his music never faded.

Today, kids and adults all over the world still dance to his songs, proving that Elvis Presley's legend will never die!

From a small-town boy to a global superstar, Elvis Presley proved that dreams can come true—one song at a time!

Made in the USA
Columbia, SC
29 March 2025